In Celebration of:

_____

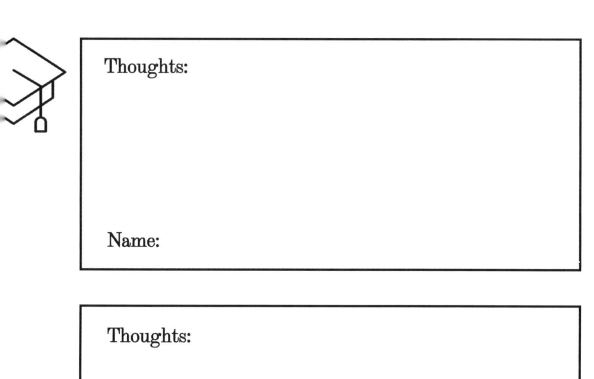

Thoughts:

Name:

Thoughts:

Name:

Thoughts:

Name:

Thoughts:

Name:

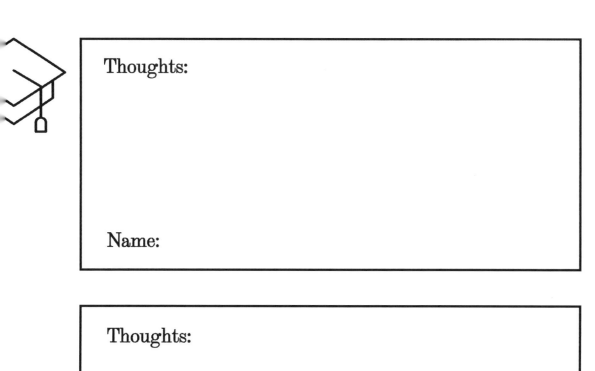

Thoughts:

Name:

Thoughts:

Name:

Thoughts:

Name:

Thoughts:

Name:

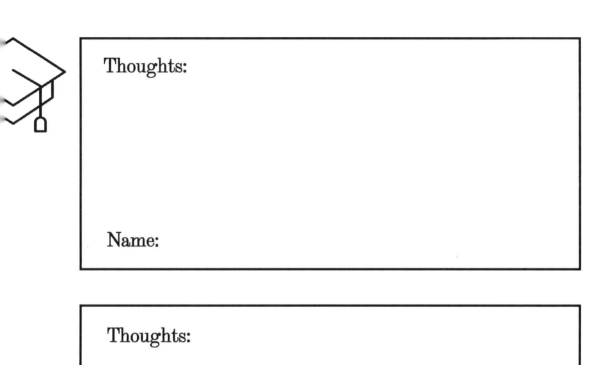

Thoughts:

Name:

Thoughts:

Name:

Thoughts:

Name:

Thoughts:

Name:

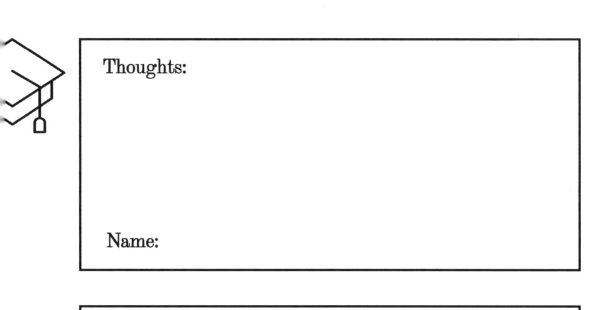

Thoughts:

Name:

Thoughts:

Name:

Thoughts:

Name:

Thoughts:

Name:

Thoughts:

Name:

Thoughts:

Name:

Thoughts:

Name:

Thoughts:

Name:

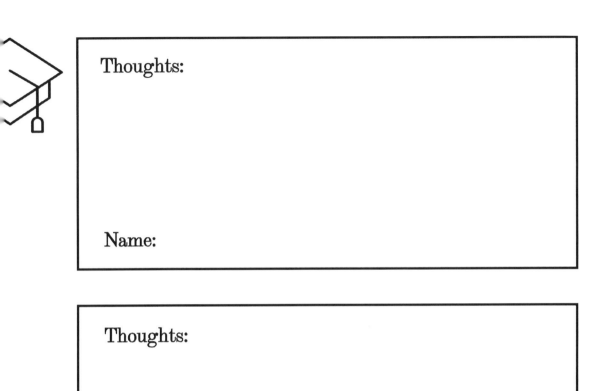

Thoughts:

Name:

Thoughts:

Name:

Thoughts:

Name:

Thoughts:

Name:

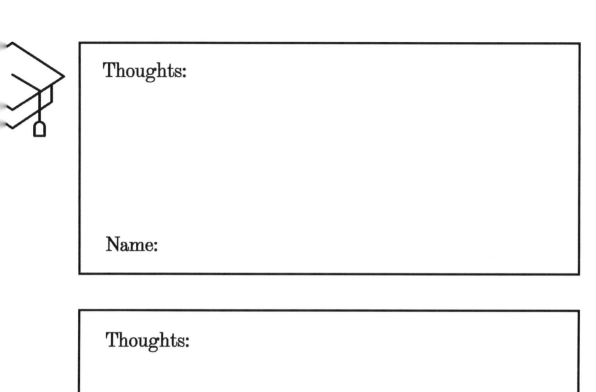

Thoughts:

Name:

Thoughts:

Name:

Thoughts:

Name:

Thoughts:

Name:

Thoughts:

Name:

Thoughts:

Name:

Thoughts:

Name:

Thoughts:

Name:

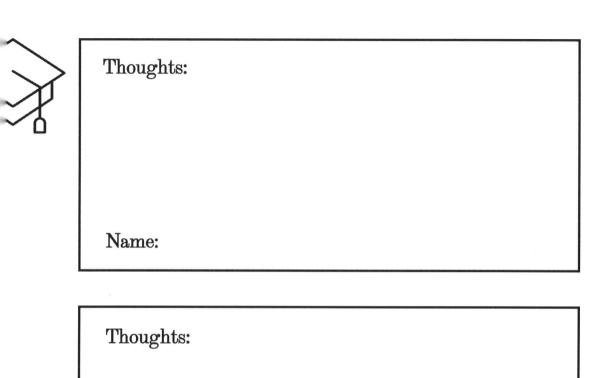

Thoughts:

Name:

Thoughts:

Name:

Thoughts:

Name:

Thoughts:

Name:

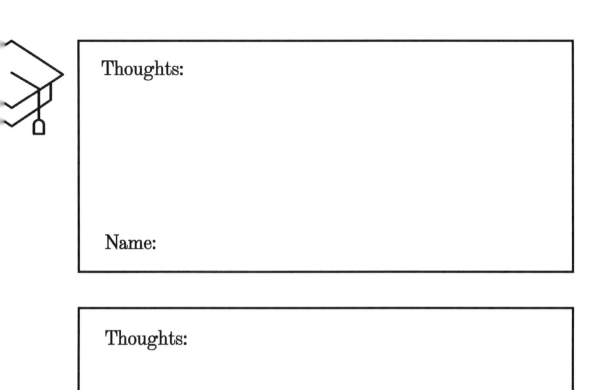

Thoughts:

Name:

Thoughts:

Name:

Thoughts:

Name:

Thoughts:

Name:

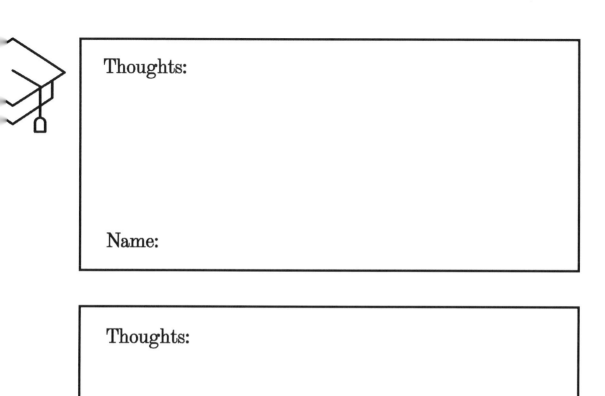

Thoughts:

Name:

Thoughts:

Name:

Thoughts:

Name:

Thoughts:

Name:

Thoughts:

Name:

Thoughts:

Name:

Thoughts:

Name:

Thoughts:

Name:

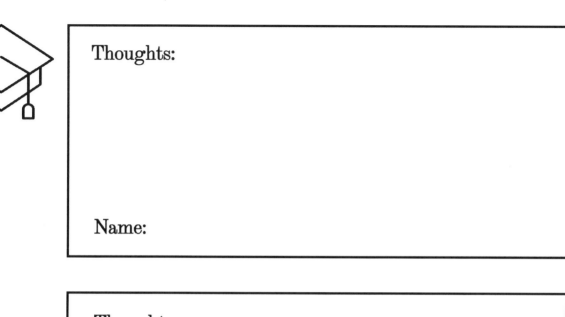

Thoughts:

Name:

Thoughts:

Name:

Thoughts:

Name:

Thoughts:

Name:

Thoughts:

Name:

Thoughts:

Name:

Thoughts:

Name:

Thoughts:

Name:

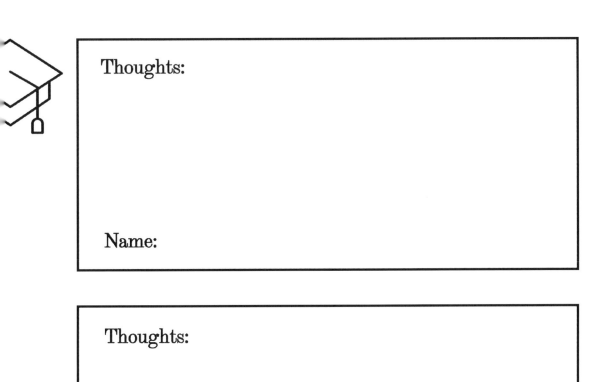

Thoughts:

Name:

Thoughts:

Name:

Thoughts:

Name:

Thoughts:

Name:

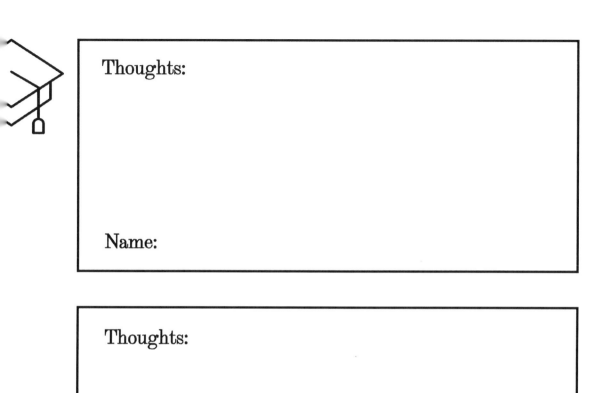

Thoughts:

Name:

Thoughts:

Name:

Thoughts:

Name:

Thoughts:

Name:

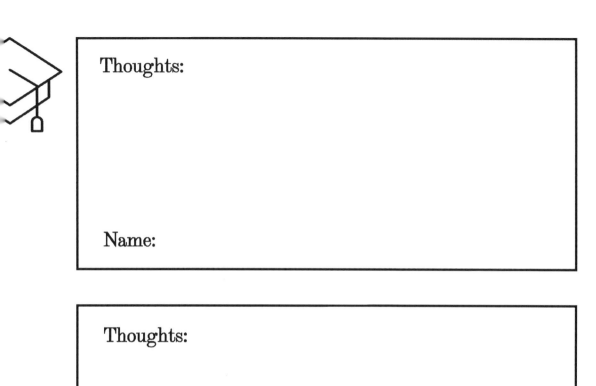

Thoughts:

Name:

Thoughts:

Name:

Thoughts:

Name:

Thoughts:

Name:

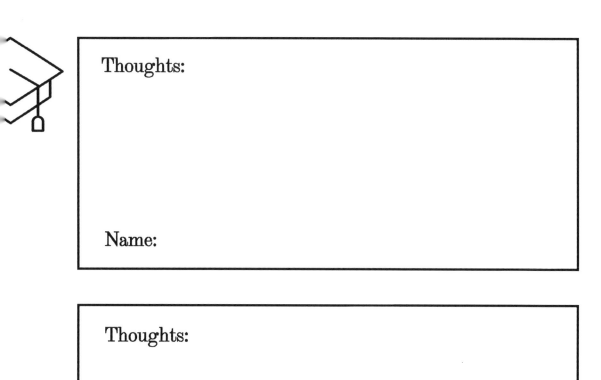

Thoughts:

Name:

Thoughts:

Name:

Thoughts:

Name:

Thoughts:

Name:

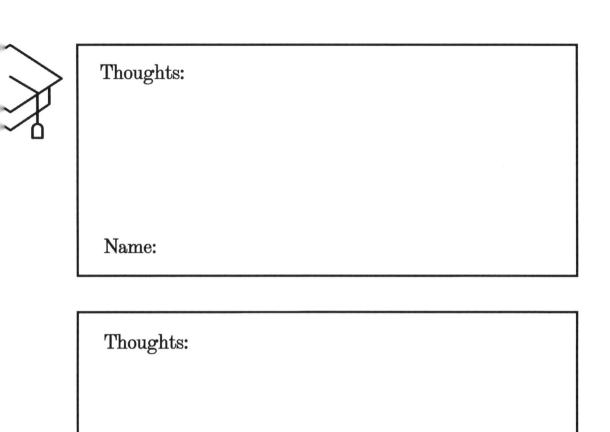

Thoughts:

Name:

Thoughts:

Name:

Thoughts:

Name:

Thoughts:

Name:

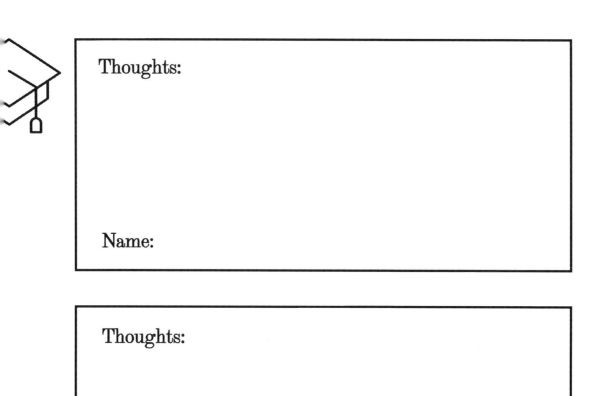

Thoughts:

Name:

Thoughts:

Name:

Thoughts:

Name:

Thoughts:

Name:

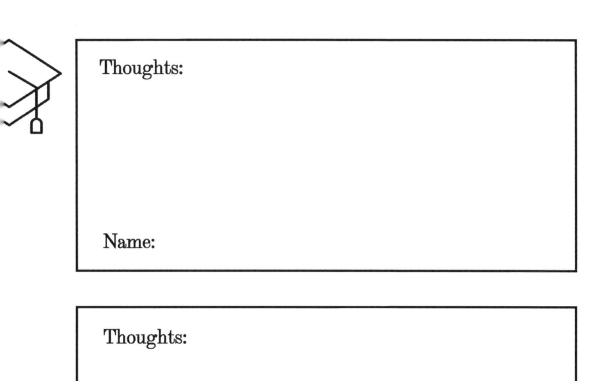

Thoughts:

Name:

Thoughts:

Name:

Thoughts:

Name:

Thoughts:

Name:

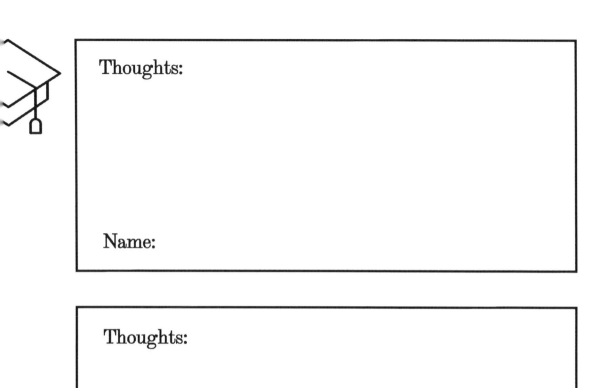

Thoughts:

Name:

Thoughts:

Name:

Thoughts:

Name:

Thoughts:

Name:

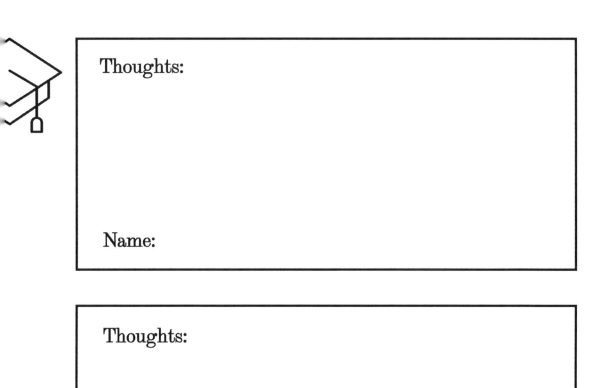

Thoughts:

Name:

Thoughts:

Name:

Thoughts:

Name:

Thoughts:

Name:

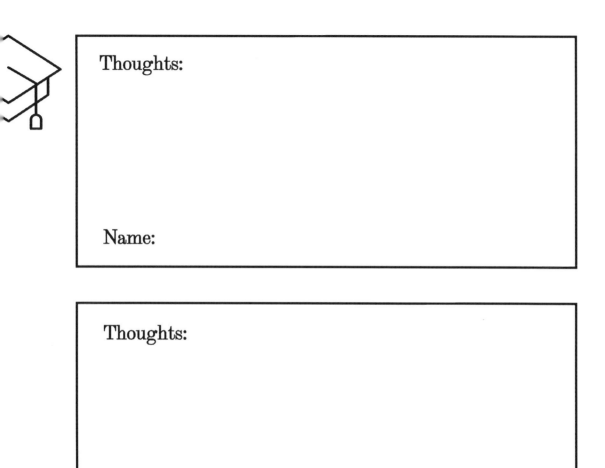

Thoughts:

Name:

Thoughts:

Name:

Thoughts:

Name:

Thoughts:

Name:

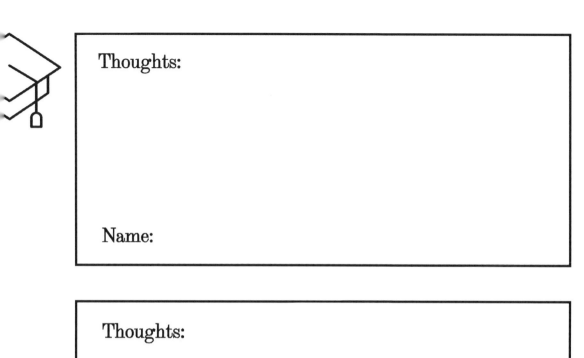

Thoughts:

Name:

Thoughts:

Name:

Thoughts:

Name:

Thoughts:

Name:

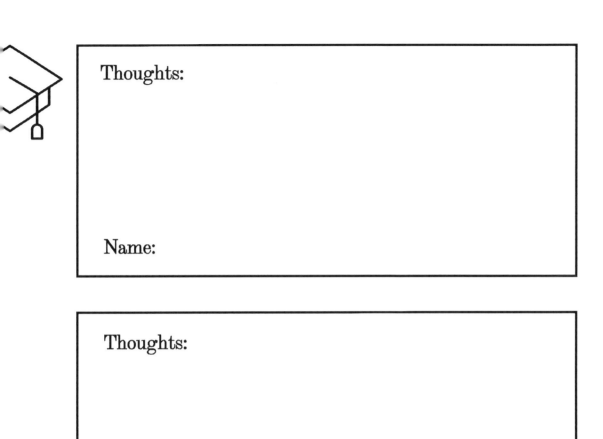

Thoughts:

Name:

Thoughts:

Name:

Thoughts:

Name:

Thoughts:

Name:

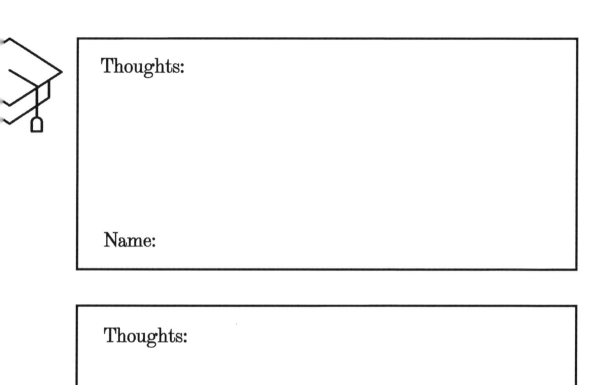

Thoughts:

Name:

Thoughts:

Name:

Thoughts:

Name:

Thoughts:

Name:

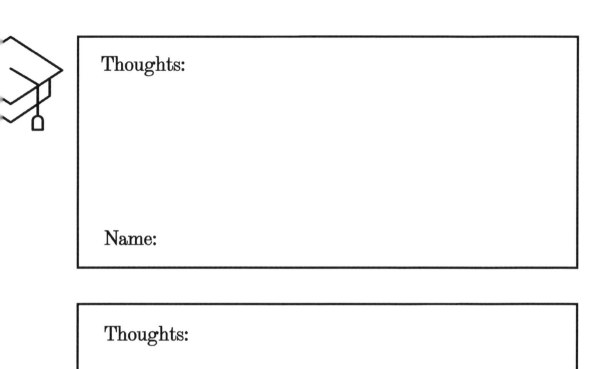

Thoughts:

Name:

Thoughts:

Name:

Thoughts:

Name:

Thoughts:

Name:

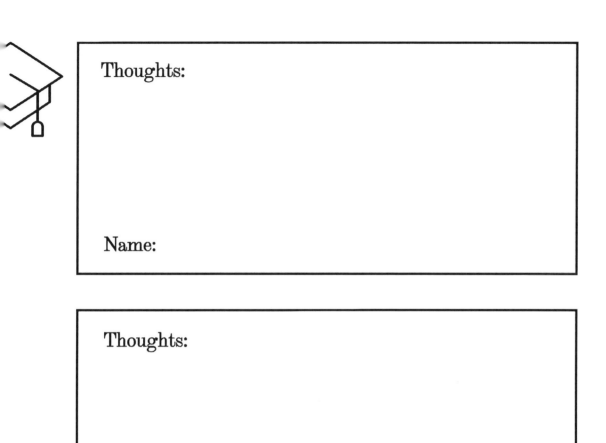

Thoughts:

Name:

Thoughts:

Name:

Thoughts:

Name:

Thoughts:

Name:

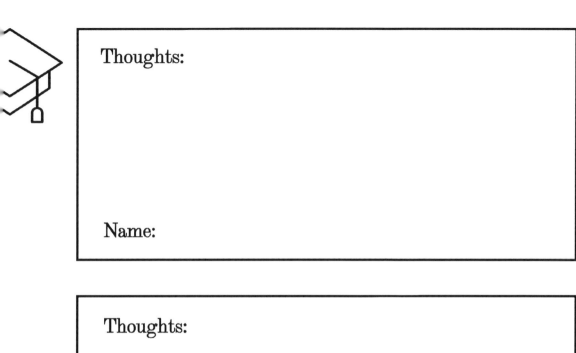

Thoughts:

Name:

Thoughts:

Name:

Thoughts:

Name:

Thoughts:

Name:

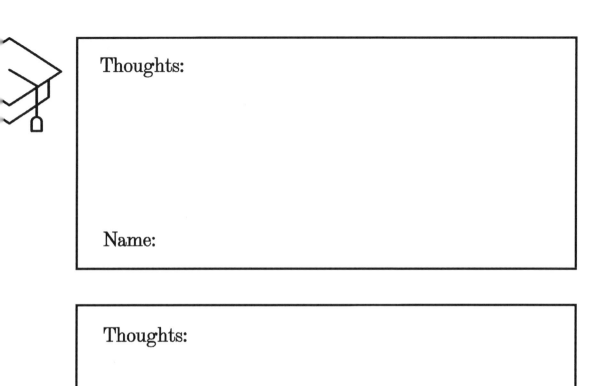

Thoughts:

Name:

Thoughts:

Name:

Thoughts:

Name:

Thoughts:

Name:

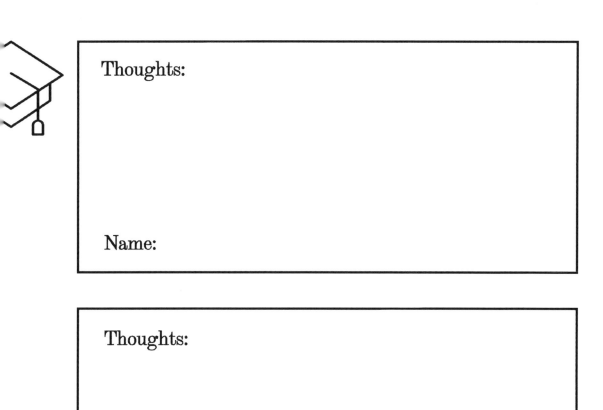

Thoughts:

Name:

Thoughts:

Name:

Thoughts:

Name:

Thoughts:

Name:

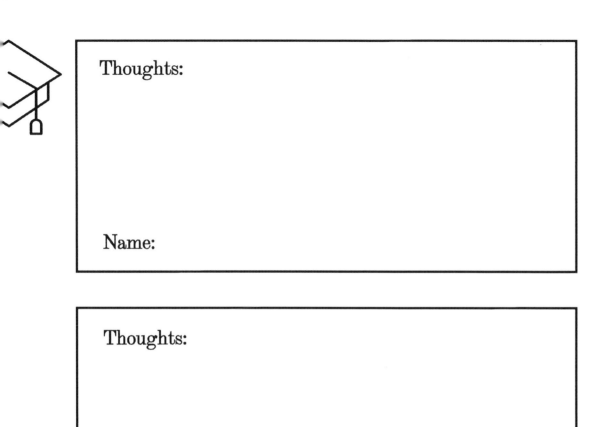

Thoughts:

Name:

Thoughts:

Name:

Thoughts:

Name:

Thoughts:

Name:

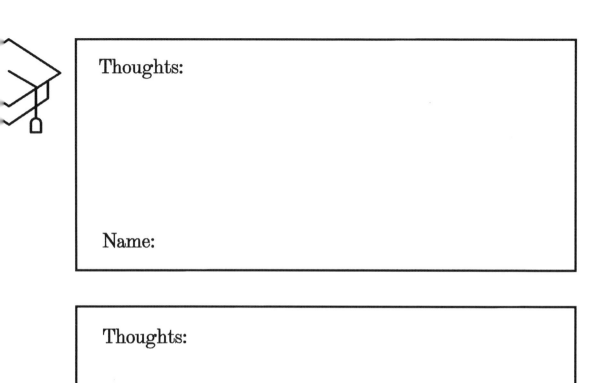

Thoughts:

Name:

Thoughts:

Name:

Thoughts:

Name:

Thoughts:

Name:

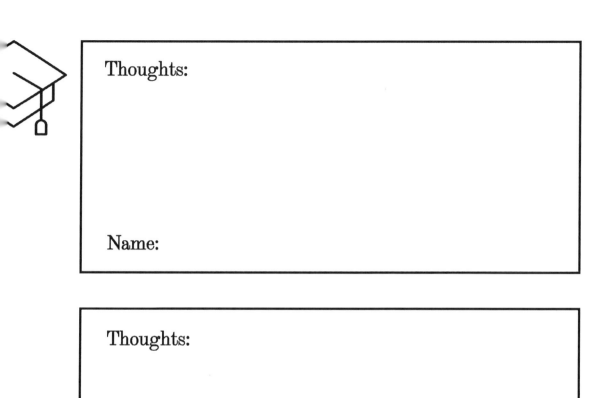

Thoughts:

Name:

Thoughts:

Name:

Thoughts:

Name:

Thoughts:

Name:

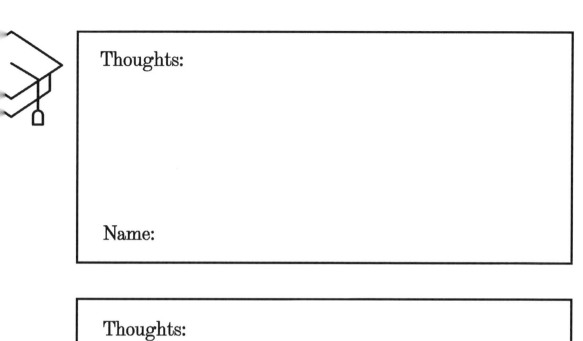

Thoughts:

Name:

Thoughts:

Name:

Thoughts:

Name:

Thoughts:

Name:

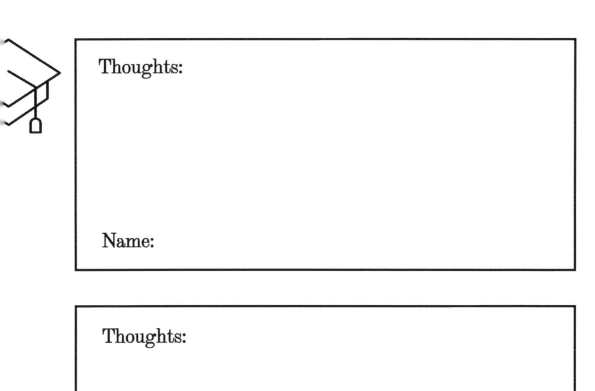

Thoughts:

Name:

Thoughts:

Name:

Thoughts:

Name:

Thoughts:

Name:

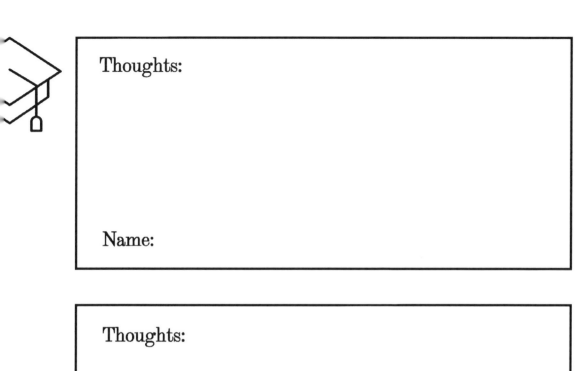

Thoughts:

Name:

Thoughts:

Name:

Thoughts:

Name:

Thoughts:

Name:

Thoughts:

Name:

Thoughts:

Name:

Thoughts:

Name:

Thoughts:

Name:

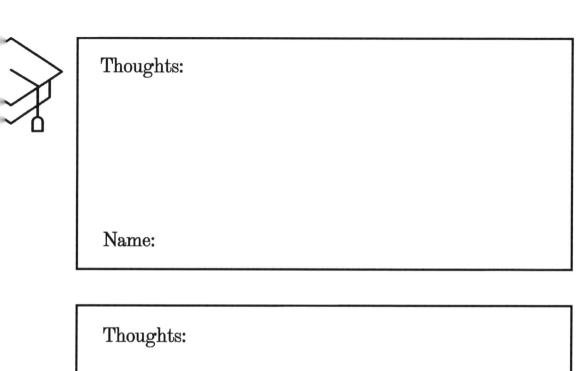

Thoughts:

Name:

Thoughts:

Name:

Thoughts:

Name:

Thoughts:

Name:

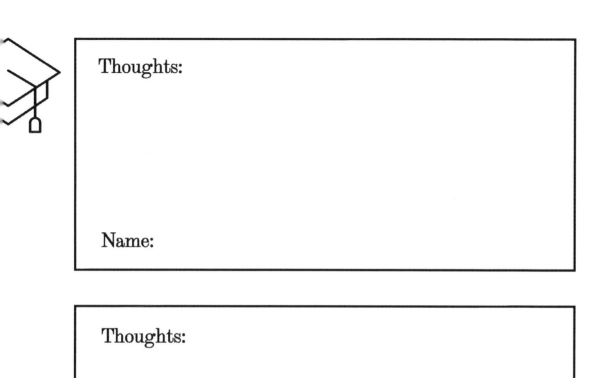

Thoughts:

Name:

Thoughts:

Name:

Thoughts:

Name:

Thoughts:

Name:

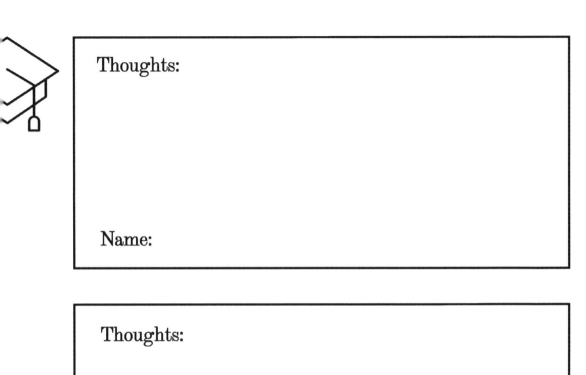

Thoughts:

Name:

Thoughts:

Name:

Thoughts:

Name:

Thoughts:

Name:

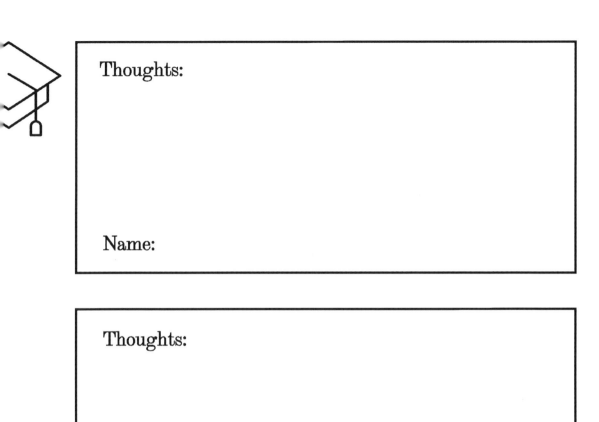

Thoughts:

Name:

Thoughts:

Name:

Thoughts:

Name:

Thoughts:

Name:

Thoughts:

Name:

Thoughts:

Name:

Thoughts:

Name:

Thoughts:

Name:

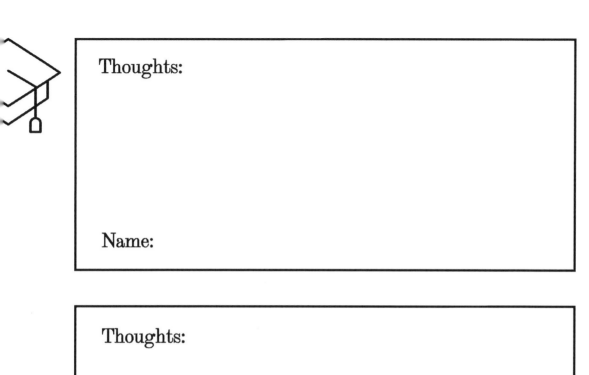

Thoughts:

Name:

Thoughts:

Name:

Thoughts:

Name:

Thoughts:

Name:

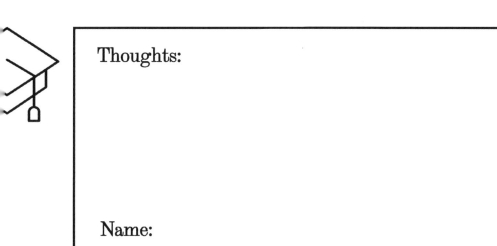

Thoughts:

Name:

Thoughts:

Name:

Thoughts:

Name:

Thoughts:

Name:

Thoughts:

Name:

Thoughts:

Name:

Thoughts:

Name:

Thoughts:

Name:

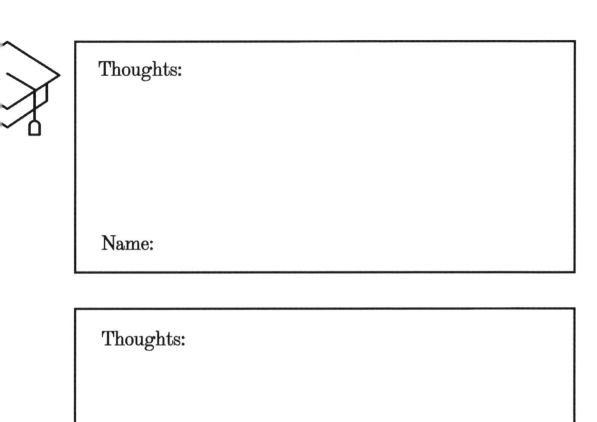

Thoughts:

Name:

Thoughts:

Name:

Thoughts:

Name:

Thoughts:

Name:

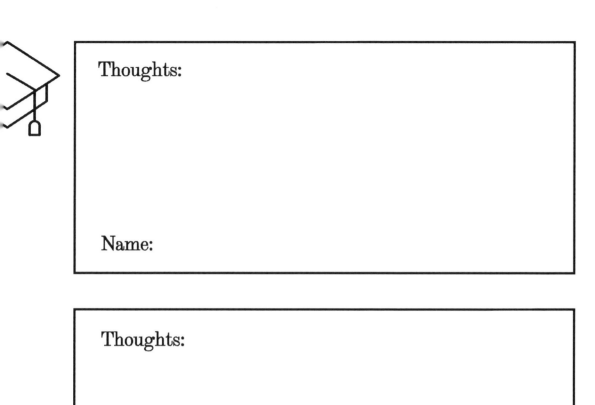

Thoughts:

Name:

Thoughts:

Name:

Thoughts:

Name:

Thoughts:

Name:

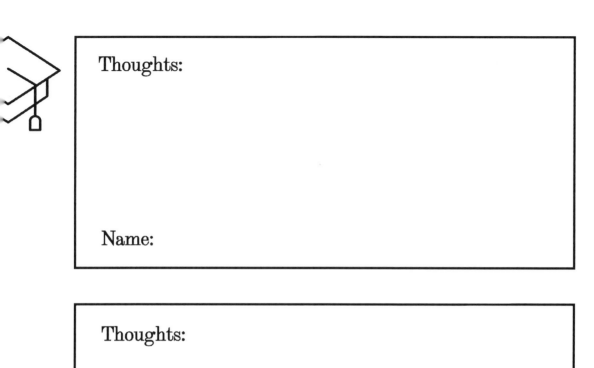

Thoughts:

Name:

Thoughts:

Name:

Thoughts:

Name:

Thoughts:

Name:

Made in the USA
Columbia, SC
14 April 2022